Pebble® Plus

Life around the World

Homes in Many Cultures

by Heather Adamson

Consulting Editor: Gail Saunders-Smith, PhD

Capstone press®

Mankato, Minnesota

Pebble Plus is published by Capstone Press,
151 Good Counsel Drive, P.O. Box 669, Mankato, Minnesota 56002.
www.capstonepub.com

 Books published by Capstone Press are manufactured with paper
containing at least 10 percent post-consumer waste.

Library of Congress Cataloging-in-Publication Data
Adamson, Heather, 1974–
    Homes in many cultures / by Heather Adamson.
    p. cm.—(Pebble plus. Life around the world)
    Summary: "Simple text and photographs present homes from many cultures"—Provided by publisher.
    Includes bibliographical references and index.
    ISBN-13: 978-1-4296-0020-0 (hardcover)
    ISBN-10: 1-4296-0020-9 (hardcover)
    ISBN-13: 978-1-4296-3380-2 (softcover)
    ISBN-10: 1-4296-3380-8 (softcover)
    1. Dwellings—Juvenile literature. I. Title. II. Series.
GT172.A43 2008
392.3'6—dc22   2006101955

Editorial Credits
Sarah L. Schuette, editor; Alison Thiele, set designer; Kara Birr, photo researcher

Photo Credits
Art Directors/Helene Rogers, 15
Folio Inc./Walter Bibikow, 19
The Image Finders/Mark E. Gibson, 11
Shutterstock/Blaz Kure, cover (Italy); czardases, 17; Lakis Fourouklas, 1 (Thailand); Marc Dietrich, 21;
    Michael G. Smith, 5; Pichugin Dmitry, 9; Simon Krzic, 7
SuperStock Inc./age fotostock, 13

Note to Parents and Teachers

The Life around the World set supports national social studies standards related to culture
and geography. This book describes and illustrates homes in many cultures. The
images support early readers in understanding the text. The repetition of words and
phrases helps early readers learn new words. This book also introduces early readers
to subject-specific vocabulary words, which are defined in the Glossary section. Early
readers may need assistance to read some words and to use the Table of Contents,
Glossary, Read More, Internet Sites, and Index sections of the book.

Printed in the United States of America in North Mankato, Minnesota.
082010   005925R

Table of Contents

Places to Live

Big or small. Flat or tall.

Homes are safe places

to rest and play.

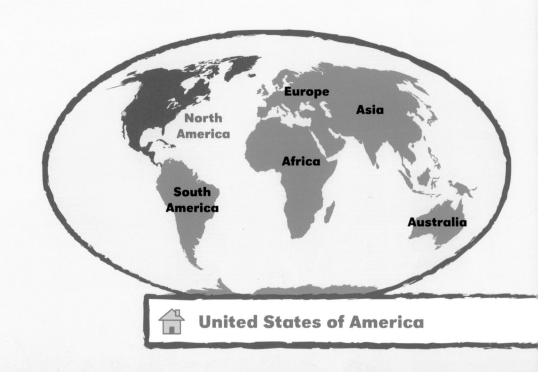

North America

Europe

Asia

Africa

South America

Australia

🏠 **United States of America**

Kinds of Homes

Cabins have thick walls
to keep out the cold.

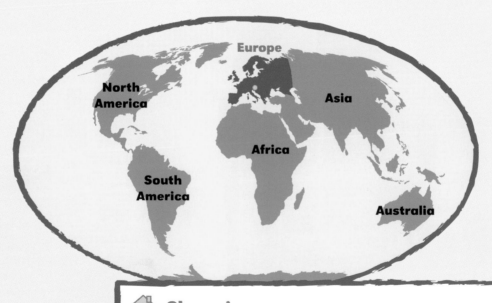

🏠 Slovenia

Huts have grass roofs
to keep off the rain.

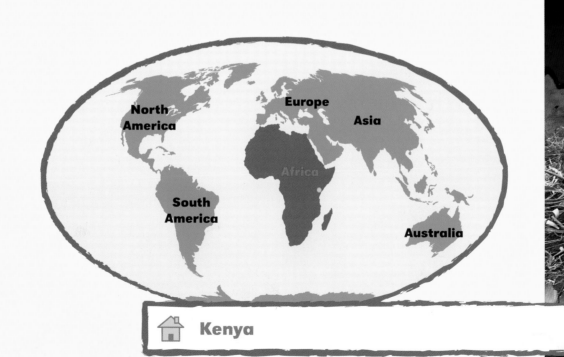

North
America

Europe

Asia

South
America

Africa

Australia

🏠 Kenya

Adobe homes
are made of clay.
Clay stays cool
in the hot desert sun.

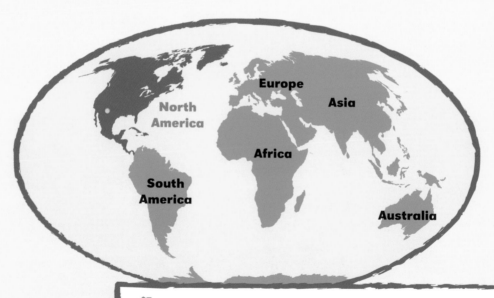

🏠 **United States of America**

Stilt houses are
built above rivers
to keep water out.

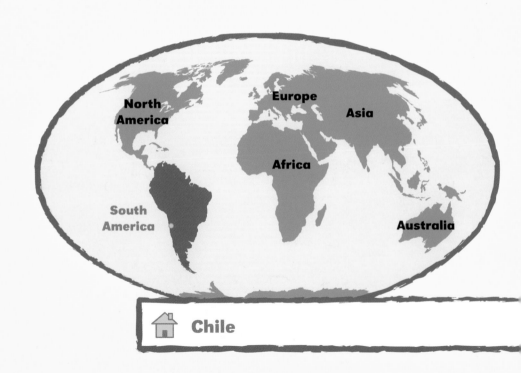

North
America

Europe

Asia

Africa

South
America

Australia

🏠 Chile

Houseboats are
floating homes that sail
up and down rivers.

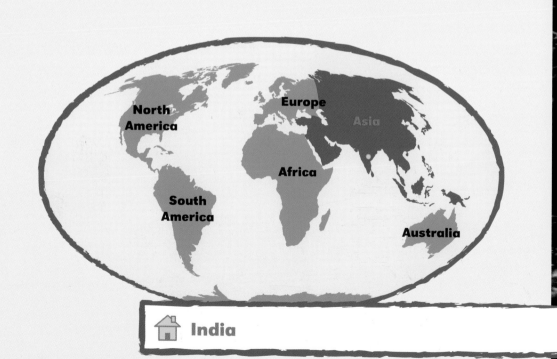

🏠 India

City and Country

Big cities have
apartment buildings
where lots of families live.

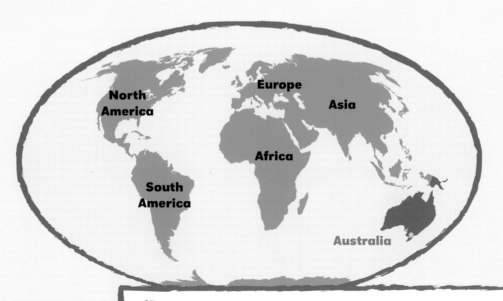

 Australia

Country farms have
lots of land where
one family's home sits.

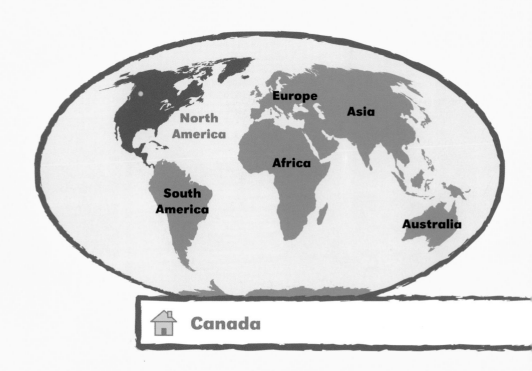

Europe

Asia

North
America

Africa

South
America

Australia

🏠 Canada

Your Home

The world has
all kinds of homes.
What's your home like?

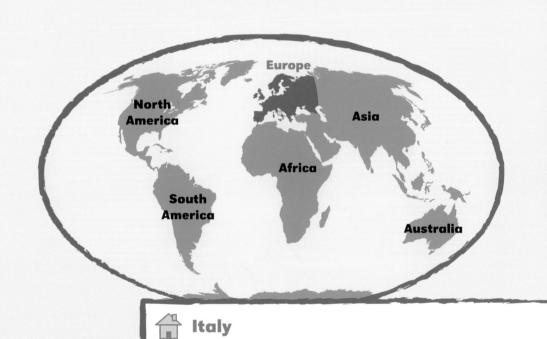

North
America

Europe

Asia

Africa

South
America

Australia

🏠 Italy

Index

Word Count: 98
Grade: 1
Early-Intervention Level: 12